A School in Every County

The Partnership of Jewish Philanthropist Julius Rosenwald & American Black Communities

"As an American and as a Jew, I appeal to all high-minded men and women to join in a relentless crusade against race prejudice, indulgence in which will result in the blotting out of the highest ideals of our proud nation."

—Julius Rosenwald, 1911

Jeffrey Sosland/author
Designed by Valerie Winer, AURAS Design, Washington, D.C.

Library of Congress Cataloging-in-Publication Data
A School in Every County—The Partnership of Jewish Philanthropist
Julius Rosenwald and American Black Communities
Library of Congress Catalogue Card Number 95-060660

Includes bibliographical references and indexes.
Contents: v. 1. Julius Rosenwald. 2. Black Education
ISBN 0-9646528-0-3

All rights reserved under International
and Pan-American Copyright Conventions
Printed in the United States of America

©1995 Economics & Science Planning
1200 18th Street, N.W.
Washington, D.C. 20036

John L. Jackson

A School in Every County

Contents

▼

Map	6
Introduction	11
Rosenwald's Background & Philosophy	14
A Remarkable Business Career	16
Rosenwald's Special Way of Giving	19
Black America in the Early 1900s	21
Rosenwald, the YMCA and Urban Blacks	26
A Strong Partnership: Booker T. Washington and Julius Rosenwald	30
A Rosenwald School in Almost Every County	33
Beyond Schools: Rosenwald Libraries, Buses, and Fellowships	42
Conclusion	51
Appendices	53
Endorsements	59
Bibliography	63
Acknowledgements	64

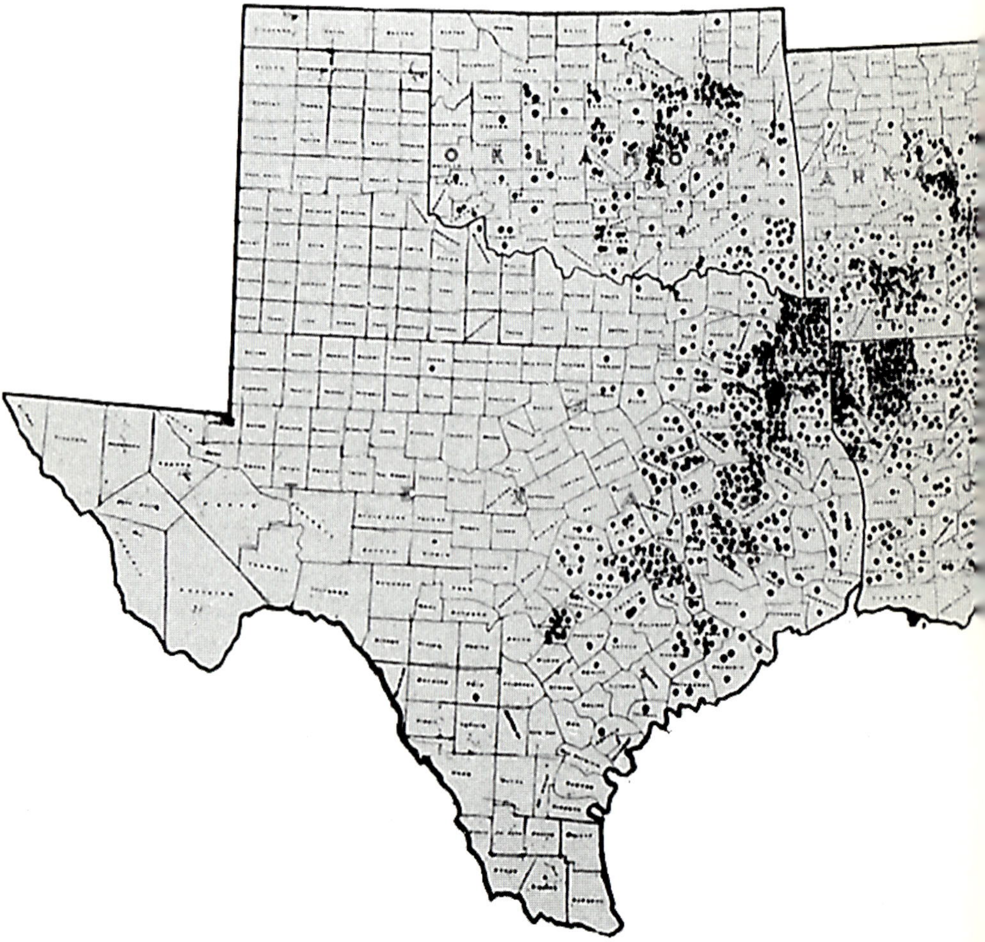

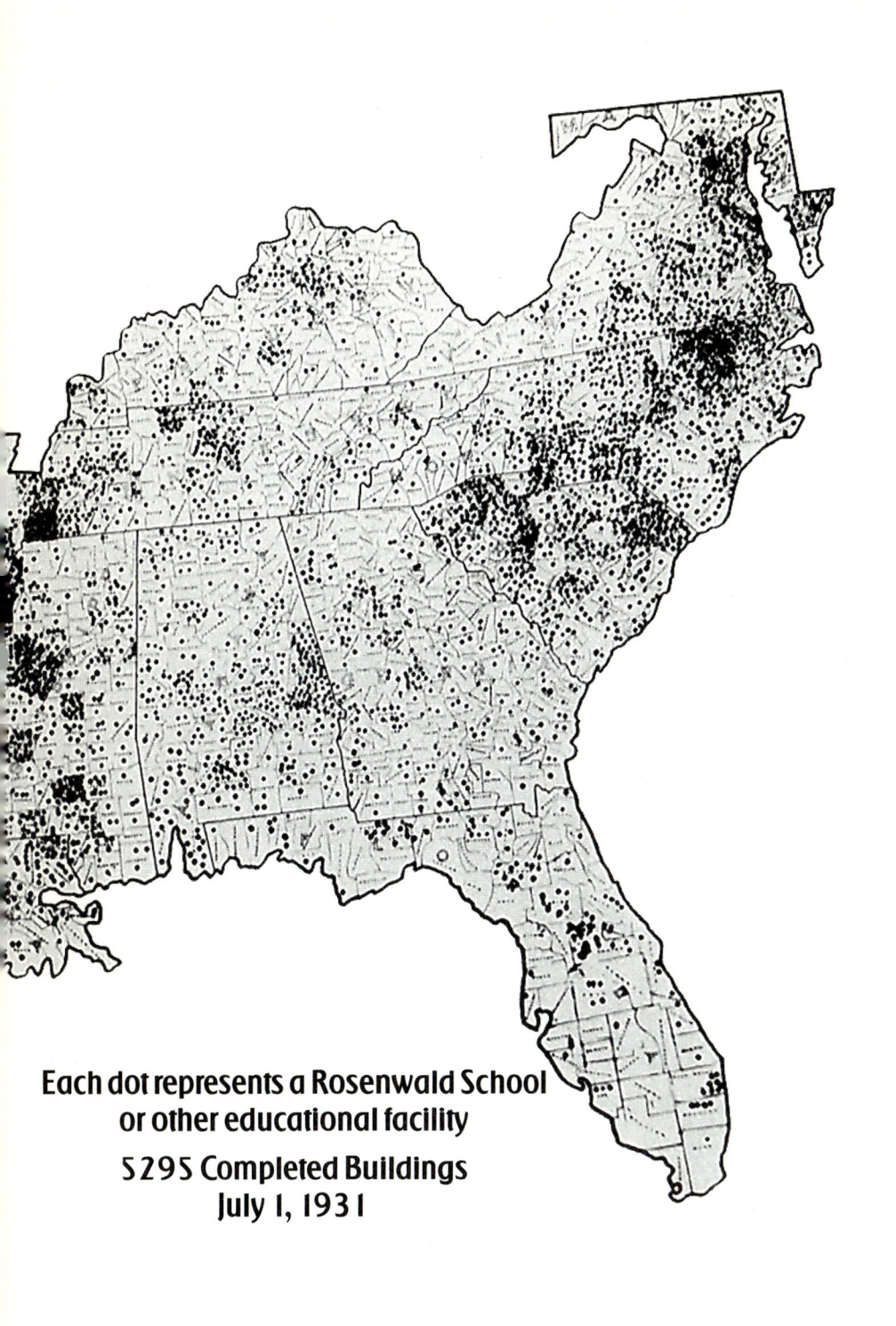

Each dot represents a Rosenwald School
or other educational facility

5295 Completed Buildings
July 1, 1931

Inserts

▼

Schoolhouse Construction
    Map of 5,295 completed buildings   6-7

Picture of Rosenwald walking with
    Washington at Tuskegee in 1915   31

Pictures from Rosenwald brochure of
    "a group of Rosenwald schools"   35
    and the "old and the new"   36

"Children's Day Program" for opening of
    Rosenwald school   38

"Rosenwald Day" Flyer   44

Introduction

▼

JULIUS ROSENWALD, STARTING IN 1912, PROVIDED THE SEED MONEY TO build more than 5,000 public schools for Southern rural Blacks and twenty-four YMCAs for urban Blacks. They were so important to the Black community that, when Rosenwald died in 1932, a prominent Black leader called him "one of the greatest friends of the Negro race since Abraham Lincoln." In the South, Rosenwald's photograph hung side by side with those of Booker T. Washington and President Abraham Lincoln on the walls of many Black schools, health clinics and homes. With the passing of this Jewish businessman, who made Sears a retail giant, grief swept the Black communities of the South, as well as the rest of America.

At a time when Federal and State governments and most philanthropic foundations neglected Black America, Rosenwald, in addition to building schools and YMCAs, contributed to medical care and training for Black doctors and nurses. Rosenwald funded bus transportation for Black students to attend rural schools, made major contributions to Black institutions of higher learning such as Tuskegee Institute, Howard, Fisk and Dillard Universities and supported libraries in schools, colleges and county seats. The

INTRODUCTION

Rosenwald Fund, which Julius Rosenwald established in 1917, also helped to create the United Negro College Fund in 1944 and Rosenwald fellowships that supported advanced study for more than 1,500 talented individuals, including W.E.B. DuBois, Ralph Bunche, Ralph Ellison, Walter White and Marian Anderson. These grants gave a generation of Black leaders the opportunity to study at some of the best institutions of higher education.

For the final twelve years of his life, Rosenwald's philanthropy was devoted to improving race relations. His programs worked to promote the growth of that segment of the population that had been most neglected. His leadership and donations served as a catalyst for raising two to five times the amount he donated and involved key members of the Black community. Rosenwald's seed money elicited matching funds from Southern states and county governments as well as from the Black and Jewish communities. Before Rosenwald's crusade, these sources had been largely untapped for Black education and welfare.

During the period 1910-32, Julius Rosenwald personally contributed—in today's equivalent funds—more than one-billion dollars, and through his matching grant program raised an additional three to five-billion dollars. More than half of this money went directly to the Black community.

Julius Rosenwald helped empower Black America with the basic tools of education and vocational skills to move from the stagnation and poverty of the post–Civil War period toward the civil rights era. Rosenwald's approach not only gave many Blacks a chance for a better future, it also gave Black communities the means they needed to organize themselves successfully. As for the Jewish community and its relations with the Black community, Rosenwald helped to set a progressive agenda that has carried through the civil rights era until today.

INTRODUCTION

Who was Julius Rosenwald? What motivated this high school drop-out to use so much of his wealth for the education and welfare of the Black community? How did he convince Southern states and counties and countless Blacks and Whites to follow his example? What lessons can Black and Jewish leaders learn from Rosenwald's close relationship with Booker T. Washington? How relevant to our nation's current needs are the following words from Rosenwald's 1911 speech at Hampton, one of America's first Black institutions of higher education?

> Race prejudice is merely destructive; it offers nothing but a hopeless warfare and a blank pessimism. A nation divided against itself cannot stand; two nations cannot live side by side at dagger's point with one another, and maintain a healthy state of progress in either. Perpetual feud destroys what is best and most helpful in both.
>
> To my mind, no man can in any way render greater service to mankind than by devoting his energy toward removal of this mighty obstacle. The destruction of race prejudice is the beginning of the higher civilization.

Rosenwald's Background and Philosophy

▼

ROSENWALD'S DEDICATION TO EQUALITY AND LIBERTY WAS ROOTED IN his personal experiences. He was born during the American Civil War (1862). His father, a German Jewish immigrant, had left his homeland because of a strong dislike of militarism and a lack of economic opportunity. He entered this country with only twenty dollars. Rosenwald grew up in Springfield, Illinois—which also had been the home of Abraham Lincoln—where his parents owned and operated a small retail store.

As an adult, Rosenwald attributed much of his social vision and passion to his active membership in the Chicago Sinai Congregation. Here he was profoundly influenced by Rabbi Emil G. Hirsch. At the turn of the century Rabbi Hirsch was widely recognized as a leading rabbi in America, an outspoken man of liberal views with a deep interest in social issues. During Rosenwald's early years as a philanthropist, Hirsch turned Rosenwald's attention from purely traditional forms of charity to more socially progressive issues. In turn, Rosenwald became an outspoken leader in the Jewish community for broad-minded Jewish support of Jewish and non-Jewish social causes. In addition to his Jewish influences, Rosenwald's concern for the plight of Blacks was galvanized by his friend Dr. Paul Sachs, a former business partner of Goldman, Sachs and Company, who had taken an interest in The Urban League and subsequently enlisted Rosenwald's support for this cause. In 1910, Sachs gave Rosenwald a biography of William Baldwin, Jr., a Boston railroad executive and a founder of The Urban League, and a copy of Booker T. Washington's *Up From Slavery*. Rosenwald later said that these two books influenced him more than anything he had ever read.

Baldwin believed that the great need of the Blacks was educational opportunity, and he devoted his life to promoting Black education in the South. Rosenwald was particularly impressed with Baldwin's contention that the fate of the Blacks was inseparably linked to the progress of the nation-at-large. Rosenwald told a group of friends:

> Whether it is because I belong to a people who have known centuries of persecution, or whether it is because I am naturally inclined to sympathize with the oppressed, I have always felt keenly for the colored race.
>
> My sympathies, however, remained more or less dormant until the book "An American Citizen"—the life of William Henry Baldwin, Jr., came to my notice....Particularly was I impressed with Mr. Baldwin's contention...that the two races must occupy one country. They have to learn probably the highest and hardest of all arts, the art of living together with decency and forbearance. Nothing will so test the sincerities of religion, our moral obligation, or even our common self-respect, as will the exigencies of this which is among the greatest of all our problems.

Rosenwald also admired Dr. Washington's rise from slavery to the presidency of Tuskegee Institute and his strong belief in hard work and personal initiative. Rosenwald and Washington soon became partners in a common cause.

A Remarkable Business Career

▼

IN 1879, WITHOUT COMPLETING HIGH SCHOOL, ROSENWALD ENTERED the clothing business as an apprentice to his uncles in New York City. Within five years he had saved enough money to open his own clothing store in New York. After this successful venture, Rosenwald moved back to Illinois to manufacture garments in Chicago, and in 1895 he, along with his brother-in-law, invested $75,000 in a company with which he had done business and which his brother-in-law felt was a promising investment—Sears, Roebuck & Company. The following year Rosenwald became vice-president of Sears, moving quickly to establish a new standard of quality control that significantly enhanced the firm's reputation and profitability. Soon after Rosenwald's entry into Sears, he initiated the policy of "Your money back if not satisfied", a radical innovation at that time. In 1901 he purchased his brother-in-law's shares and four years later, with the help of his boyhood friend, Henry Goldman of Goldman, Sachs & Company, Rosenwald floated a stock issue that transformed Sears into a sizable public corporation.

Rosenwald was a pioneer in the field of mail order merchandising, instituting new systems to assure that Sears' catalog orders were processed promptly. In particular, his system called for incoming orders to be weighed to determine how many clerks would be needed to process them. By 1906, when Sears moved into a vast new plant in Chicago, orders were averaging 20,000 a day; 100,000 a day during the Christmas season. Each day of the week was assigned an order slip of its own color, so orders that had been delayed would stand out and receive quick attention. Conveyer belts and gravity chutes were installed to speed the flow of orders and merchandise, bringing everything together at an assembly point. Henry Ford was so impressed with the system that the following year he adapted the assembly line principle to automobile manufacturing, revolutionizing modern industry.

When Richard Sears retired in 1908, Rosenwald became president and quickly opened scores of mail order centers across the country. By 1909, Sears was recording annual sales of more than $50 million. Under the direction of Rosenwald, Sears became the largest mail-order house in the world.

Julius Rosenwald turned Sears, Roebuck from a shapeless, inefficient company into a rapidly expanding retailing giant. This accomplishment was recognized by his peers at the famous Pioneers of American Industry dinner in 1928. The eight men honored were: George Eastman, photography; Henry Ford, automobiles; Orville Wright and Glen Curtis, aviation; Thomas Edison, inventions; Charles Schwab, iron and steel; Harvey S. Firestone, rubber; and Julius Rosenwald, merchandising.

Although he amassed a large fortune, Rosenwald's attitude was that of a man who never regarded the money as his own. He looked upon himself as a public servant, temporarily the trustee of wealth that must, in some way, be used for the common good. He said "it is almost always easier to make a million dollars honestly than to dispose of it wisely." The habits that made him a successful businessman were used in his philanthropy. Although he gave away millions of dollars, he was watchful of budgets and pennies. He considered social projects with the same realism he applied to choosing a new line of goods for Sears. And his imagination could be stirred only on the basis of concrete projects carefully worked out and budgeted. On the other hand, he was never afraid of new ideas or new methods in social welfare any more than in industry.

Rosenwald's Special Way of Giving

▼

JULIUS ROSENWALD ADOPTED ANDREW CARNEGIE'S PHILOSOPHY OF CIVIC stewardship. Rosenwald was concerned with the massive urbanization and industrialization at the turn of the century that produced social problems and weakened the fabric of traditional American democracy. Liberty and equality were of critical importance to Rosenwald, and he wanted to guarantee that they remained an integral part of American society.

Many of Rosenwald's gifts were made through the Julius Rosenwald Fund, created in 1917, chartered simply for the "well-being of mankind." Rosenwald was adamantly opposed to placing funds in perpetuity. He strongly believed that one generation cannot foresee the needs and demands of future generations. Rosenwald stipulated that all the capital and interest in his Fund must be expended within twenty-five years after his death, and the Fund liquidated. Thus Rosenwald and his Fund made larger donations than other foundations with more sizeable endowments, because most foundations donate only the interest from their capital.

Other philanthropists had been interested in Black education well before Rosenwald appeared on the scene. Julius Rosenwald brought to the movement for Black schools a crusading zeal and

Rosenwald's Special Way of Giving

unflagging interest that stimulated public expenditures and cooperation to a level previously unknown.

Much of Rosenwald's giving was to stimulate public agencies to assume a larger share of the overall responsibility. Long before the days of the New Deal—as far back as 1915—he recognized clearly that in a modern, complex society the state must increasingly assume the burdens of education, health and a multitude of other functions that in a simpler era were supported by private charity.

While there were others who had given enormous sums to aid American Blacks, none gave so generously of themselves. Southern Blacks did not know the great philanthropist John D. Rockefeller, but many of them shook hands with Julius Rosenwald and listened to his encouraging speeches. He personally congratulated thousands of Blacks for successfully completing the funding campaign for construction of YMCAs and rural schools.

Rosenwald was also an important contributor to other educational and civic organizations. For example, he gave $3.6 million to the Joint Distribution Committee in an effort to aid the persecuted Jews of Eastern Europe and Russia. He supported a relief fund for post–World War I German children. For many years he served as the President of the Jewish Charities for Chicago and as a trustee of the University of Chicago. He was a large donor to Harvard University and a founder of the Chicago Museum of Science and Industry.

Rosenwald eventually gave away $63 million (between one and two-billion dollars in today's equivalent funds)[1] for social improvement and educational activities, and nearly half of that went to Black causes.

[1] **MIT Professor and Nobel Laureate in Economics, Robert M. Solow,** has prepared a brief memorandum in Appendix A on various approaches to calculate today's equivalent dollars from the amounts given in earlier time frames. The dollar amounts within the parentheses throughout this monograph represent a low estimate of the equivalent in today's funds. They are intended to give the reader a better idea of the real dollar values. These numbers are based on the Labor Department's Consumer Price Index, which is provided in Appendix A. The CPI for the year in which the funds were given is used to determine its equivalent in today's funds for the dollar amount within the parentheses. Therefore, the multiplier is correlated with the year the donation was made.

Black America
In The
Early 1900s

▼

DURING SLAVERY, PLANTATION OWNERS MADE A CONCERTED effort to prevent Blacks from obtaining an education in order to maintain greater control over them. Some Whites even believed that it was ordained by God that Black slaves should remain in a state of ignorance. Prior to the Civil War, almost the entire Black population was illiterate. When the War broke out, many slaves escaped, and many others were abandoned with the approach of the Union armies. The Blacks crowded into the Union Army camps, and it was there that the first systematic effort was undertaken to educate the former slave population. In 1861, the American Missionary Association organized a school for Blacks in Virginia, and in the years following the Civil War other religious and humanitarian groups took up the task. This preliminary work was valuable, but it lacked the broad, coordinated scope of a nationwide action.

During the Reconstruction era, due to political pressure and Black representation, some funds were appropriated for Black schools by the Southern states. However, the war-torn South could not afford decent public education, even for favored Whites, much less for the Black population. Of course all White schools were segregated and no Blacks could attend. Black public schools that existed were located in old churches, ramshackle huts, lodge halls and small, rented homes. These structures were dilapidated and totally inadequate for educational use.

After the Reconstruction period, White political control was completely reestablished, and Blacks were virtually disenfranchised throughout the South. They were socially ostracized and economically deprived.

After the Civil War, a few institutions of higher education and manual training were established for Blacks, such as Fisk University in Tennessee, Howard University in Washington, D.C., and Atlanta University in Georgia. Despite this, Black illiteracy in 1870 was estimated to be 80 percent. Ten years later, the Alabama legislature passed a law establishing the Tuskegee Normal and Industrial Institute. Booker T. Washington opened Tuskegee as the only teacher in a rented shanty church with 30 pupils.

Soon after his arrival in Alabama, Dr. Washington toured the rural districts near Tuskegee and found the school system to be wretched. The schools lacked the most basic facilities. Schools met only three to five months a year and most teachers lacked formal training. Dr. Washington believed the salvation of Blacks lay in education and advocated needed improvements for schools. Furthermore, the attitude of Whites had to change because, as Washington put it, "You cannot hold a man in a ditch without standing in the ditch with him."

Dr. Washington recognized that 85 percent of the Gulf states' population depended on agriculture for their livelihood. Therefore, he sought to teach his students marketable agricultural skills. He needed funding for such an ambitious undertaking, but the State of Alabama provided only $3,000 ($52,000). There was no Federal money for Dr. Washington's program, so he went North to raise money from private institutions.

By 1908, various educational foundations began funding agricultural education and rural schools. Traveling teachers funded by the Rockefeller Foundation aroused the local Black communities' interest in improving rural schools. With limited resources, these foundations attempted to do what the Federal and State governments had ignored.

Eighty percent of American Blacks (who then numbered ten million or 11 percent of the American population) were still concentrated in the South and most worked at menial tasks. The largest barrier to equal opportunity and racial justice remained White intolerance. Contemporary editors of the *Encyclopedia Britannica* explained that the "Negro" had a "less voluminous brain as compared with the White races," was "on a lower evolutionary plane than the White man," and was "more closely related to the highest anthropoids." "After puberty," the encyclopedia concluded, "sexual matters take the first place in the Negro's life and thoughts." Racial prejudice was also prevalent in Europe, but there Jews were the targets.

Disenfranchisement and false genetic propaganda were only some forms of racial discrimination suffered by Blacks. Schools in 1910 spent approximately $2.20 ($34.38) per Black pupil annually, while the amount spent for Southern Whites was more than double that, $4.90 ($76.56), and for the nation at large it was $21.15 ($330.47). The illiteracy of Blacks in some states was still as high as 50 percent, four to five times that of Southern Whites. Three-fourths of Blacks were tenants or share-croppers, with an annual wage of approximately $100 ($1,500), with thousands held to the land by contract labor systems that amounted to serfdom. Dr. Washington privately funded the legal struggle against this practice.

When Blacks complained, many in the South resorted to lynching. During the first decade of the twentieth century, an average of 93 lynchings occurred per year.

Black America In The Early 1900s

Some Northerners and most Southerners regularly endorsed racial discrimination, viewing Blacks as children in need of protection and as a biologically inferior race. In the face of such attitudes, it is not surprising that the self-help philosophy of Booker T. Washington was popular among Blacks during this period. He believed that through education and training Black America could make social and economic progress. To Dr. Washington, "the opportunity to earn a dollar in a factory just now is worth infinitely more than the opportunity to spend a dollar in an opera-house." Dr. Washington believed the first priority of his people should be self-help. Indeed, the harsh conditions in the South influenced many Blacks in that era to adopt this pragmatic view toward equality, as to what was achievable in the near term, and what was not. Nonetheless, economic and social equality was the final objective.

Not all Blacks agreed with Dr. Washington, and in the early 1900s, men like W.E.B. Du Bois began rebelling against his leadership. A product of the middle class, Du Bois was raised in Massachusetts and educated at Fisk and Harvard, where he received his Ph.D. in 1895 and where he was dismayed by racial slurs. He joined others to demand equality immediately. He criticized Washington's methods as being too passive. In 1909, he co-founded the NAACP. This interracial organization did not demand social mixing of the races, or total integration—which few blacks or whites wanted. However, it did seek to overturn the legal and economic barriers to equal opportunity. Unlike Du Bois, Washington lived in the difficult South and understood that the war against inequality had to be fought one battle at a time. "The agitation of questions of social equality," Washington insisted, "is the extremist's folly, and progress in the enjoyment of all the privileges that will come to us must be the result of severe constant struggle rather than of artificial forcing."

Julius Rosenwald sided with Dr. Washington. Even as the new president of Sears, Rosenwald was thwarted in his attempts to alter the discriminatory practices in his own firm and in the Chicago office buildings he owned. His associates, employees and tenants would not agree to give Blacks increased opportunities for employment. Once he understood that he was creating antagonism against the very people he was trying to help, he directed his efforts toward ensuring educational opportunities, in the belief that it would ultimately lead to the end of discrimination and bring about equality for Blacks.

Rosenwald, the YMCA and Urban Blacks

▼

BY 1910 JULIUS ROSENWALD HAD BECOME THE PRESIDENT OF Sears, had read Baldwin's and Washington's books and was anxious to focus on the plight of Blacks. Responding to employment opportunities in the North—especially during World War I—nearly one million Blacks migrated from the South between 1910 and 1920. The Black population in northern cities increased by 35 percent in these years. Racial intolerance toward Blacks existed in the North as well as the South resulting in the establishment of Black ghettos in the cities of the North. Nevertheless, migration to the North, into blue-collar manufacturing jobs, offered thousands of disadvantaged Blacks a better life than they had previously known.

Rosenwald met in 1910 with the YMCA leadership, who were in the midst of a fund-raising campaign to build YMCAs for urban Blacks. Rosenwald surprised the group by offering to contribute the generous sum of $25,000 ($390,000) to every community in the United States that raised $75,000 ($1.17 million) toward the construction of YMCAs in Black neighborhoods. About 40 Black YMCAs existed in American cities; however, none had modern buildings designed and built for YMCA use. Instead they usually functioned in rented premises, often former saloons or old buildings converted into YMCA facilities.

Rosenwald decided to support the YMCA because its programs provided Blacks with opportunities to help themselves and to achieve personal improvement without charity. He believed that charity undermines personal initiative and deprives individuals of the sense of pride and achievement that can only be gained through hard work. Other philanthropists previously had donated money for construction of YMCAs in Washington, D.C., and Columbus, Georgia, but Black participation had not been a precondition for either project. The value of Rosenwald's method of giving was to elicit participation. He stipulated that part of the funds must be raised by Blacks, and it was one of the first times that Black urban communities had an opportunity to manage and contribute to so large an enterprise. They seized the opportunity. In Philadelphia, $23,000 ($360,000) was collected in only six days and in Nashville $33,000 ($515,000) was raised in only nine days.

When the YMCA leadership explained to Rosenwald that only Protestants could be associated with the YMCA's management, he responded:

> I want nothing to do with the management. I have been studying the colored people and have come to the conclusion that they need help more than any other group, and I want to help them and encourage other rich Jews to do the same thing. I believe that the Young Men's Christian Association is the best medium I know for accomplishing what I would like to see done for colored men, and this does not mean that I am any less a Jew.

The public announcement of Rosenwald's offer won instant approval throughout the United States. Among those who wrote to congratulate him was President Taft, who invited him to the White House and solicited Rosenwald for money to complete Washington's YMCA. Rosenwald agreed enthusiastically to the proposal.

Rosenwald's offer triggered nationwide fund-raising campaigns and resulted in the construction of 24 YMCA buildings. These were equipped with swimming pools, gymnasia, cafeterias, reading rooms and classrooms, employment bureaus, and dormitories. They provided facilities previously all but unknown to Blacks. The pools and gyms offered recreation and exercise for YMCA members as well as for Black students from area schools. The YMCA educational program included a variety of classes, such as elementary English, typing, architectural drawing, stenography, auto mechanics and driving lessons that could enhance the vocational qualifications of members. For a long time the dormitories of the Rosenwald YMCAs were practically the only places where Black male travelers could find comfortable and safe sleeping accommodations.

By 1933, the 24 Rosenwald YMCAs had an aggregate membership of almost 20,000. The location of these YMCAs in or near Black business districts enhanced their importance to the Black community. Successful fund-raising drives also brought the Black community together, gave it greater self-confidence, and inspired other activities for community welfare. By providing recreational and educational programs as well as accommodations, the YMCA offered Blacks the first real alternative to the city streets. In the end, over 24 communities took advantage of the offer, and Rosenwald's total contribution grew to $700,000 ($5.9 million). But even more impressive was the fact that communities across the country rose to the challenge and raised over $6 million ($50.8 million) for YMCAs (Appendix B is a list of Rosenwald YMCAs).

Rosenwald addressed the opening of the Chicago YMCA:

The man who hates a Black man because he is Black has the same spirit as he who hates a poor man because he is poor. It is the spirit of caste. I am the inferior of any man whose rights I trample under my feet.

Men are not superior by the accident of race or color; they are superior who have the best heart, the best brain. Superiority is born of honesty of virtue, of charity, and above all, of love of liberty.

Of one thing you colored men can rest assured; the most intelligent, the grandest are on your side. The sympathies of the noblest are with you. Your enemies are also the enemies of liberty, of progress and of justice.

The White men who make the White race honorable believe in equal rights for you.

A Strong Partnership:
Booker T. Washington and Julius Rosenwald

▼

IN 1911, LESS THAN A YEAR AFTER THE INITIATION OF THE YMCA fundraising drive, Booker T. Washington came to Chicago to raise money for the Tuskegee Institute. Rosenwald jumped at the opportunity to meet him and organized a luncheon for Dr. Washington, inviting bankers and other businessmen, educators and public officials.

In introducing Washington, Rosenwald said:

> The wise, statesmanlike leader who is our guest today, is greatly serving two races, which, but for his ministry of conciliation, might drift into irreconcilable antagonism. He is helping his own race to attain the high art of self-help and self-dependence, and he is helping the white race to learn that opportunity and obligation go hand in hand, and that there is no enduring superiority save that which comes from the result of serving. His own rise from slavery as told by him with simplicity and truth, to the place of guide of one race, and friend and counselor of two races, is prophetic of the widening opportunities of his people. Happy the race which follows his sane, wise, earnest leadership!

Julius Rosenwald & Booker T. Washington
Tuskegee, 1/22/15

A Strong Partnership

Four months later Rosenwald hired a private railroad car and took a party of relatives and friends, including his rabbi, Emil G. Hirsch, to the Tuskegee Institute. A meeting was held in the chapel with the faculty and about 2,000 students. Rosenwald told those gathered that he was "inspired beyond words" and wished other men could see the level of education achieved at Tuskegee. He had enormous admiration for Dr. Washington, and they developed a warm friendship.

Rosenwald was elected a Tuskegee trustee in February of 1912 and remained in that post for the rest of his life. One of his first acts was to take steps to relieve Dr. Washington from his continuous travel to raise funds for Tuskegee so that Dr. Washington could spend more time improving the Institute. In addition to his own contributions, Rosenwald also solicited funds from other Jewish philanthropists in New York and Chicago.

Rosenwald's entire family took great interest in Tuskegee and soon became familiar visitors to the Institute. Mr. and Mrs. Rosenwald were particularly fond of the Children's House and the kindergarten, and they paid two-thirds of the cost of maintaining this facility, which had been closed due to lack of funds. They also paid tuition for those children whose parents could not afford it.

When the Rosenwalds' rail cars backed into the small station at the Institute for their annual visit, a large group of students and faculty was always waiting to meet them. When they arrived at night, they were greeted with a torch procession and a brass band and led through the campus. During their stay the Rosenwald group would attend classes and observe students demonstrating their vocational skills.

At a time when the Ku Klux Klan was politically and socially powerful, Rosenwald was criticized by some Whites for "wasting" his money on a race that could not possibly be educated and for not using it for better causes such as "building more court houses and jails" in the South. The KKK leadership went so far as to accuse the merchandising titan Rosenwald of being a communist because he was a proponent of improved Black education and welfare.

A Rosenwald School in Almost Every County

▼

IN 1912 ROSENWALD GAVE DR. WASHINGTON A GIFT OF $25,000 ($373,000) to be used at his discretion "for the improvement and elevation of schools for Negroes." Most of this money went to off-shoots of Tuskegee, but a surplus of $2,100 ($31,000) was used to stimulate White and Black citizens to raise funds to provide a rural schoolhouse for Black children. This project had been started at Tuskegee by H.H. Rogers of Standard Oil Company but had been interrupted by his death in 1909.

After many discussions with Dr. Washington, Rosenwald agreed to the use of the surplus money for building rural schools in Alabama counties near the Institute. Both recognized a need to stimulate the communities to participate in the project.

Rosenwald was especially taken by Dr. Washington's statement on school buildings in his autobiography.

> My experience is that there is something in human nature which always makes an individual recognize and reward merit, no matter under what color of skin merit is found. I have found, too, that it is the visible, the tangible,

that goes a long way in softening prejudices. The actual sight of a first-class house that a Negro has built is ten times more potent than pages of discussion about a house that he ought to build, or perhaps could build.

Rosenwald heartily agreed with Washington that an individual who has the capability to accomplish needed tasks will succeed regardless of race or religion. Nevertheless, Rosenwald was not naive. He understood the social and economic discrimination that Blacks would endure even when educated.

The conditions of rural education for Blacks were shocking. In Alabama, where Blacks were one-half the population, only 20 percent of the Black children were enrolled in schools, as compared with 60 percent of the White children. No Black rural schools operated for longer than five months during the year; the average was about four months, as compared with a seven-month term for the White children. One of Washington's famous and pointed remarks on this matter was: "The Negro boy is smart, but White folks expect too much of him if they think he can learn as much in three months of school as their boys can in eight."

The school buildings for Black children were appalling, the teachers were poorly paid, and elementary school education was minimal. Rosenwald felt it was dangerous and wrong for ten million citizens of the United States to grow up in ignorance.

The school-building program was carried out by Clinton J. Calloway of Tuskegee, under the personal direction of Booker T. Washington. Calloway traveled through the countryside, exhorting Blacks to give money for their local schools. He stimulated support of schoolhouse construction

A Group of Rosenwald School Houses

Welsh School Jeff Davis Parish

Macedonia School Lincoln Parish

Brown School East Baton Rouge

Winnfield School Winn Parish

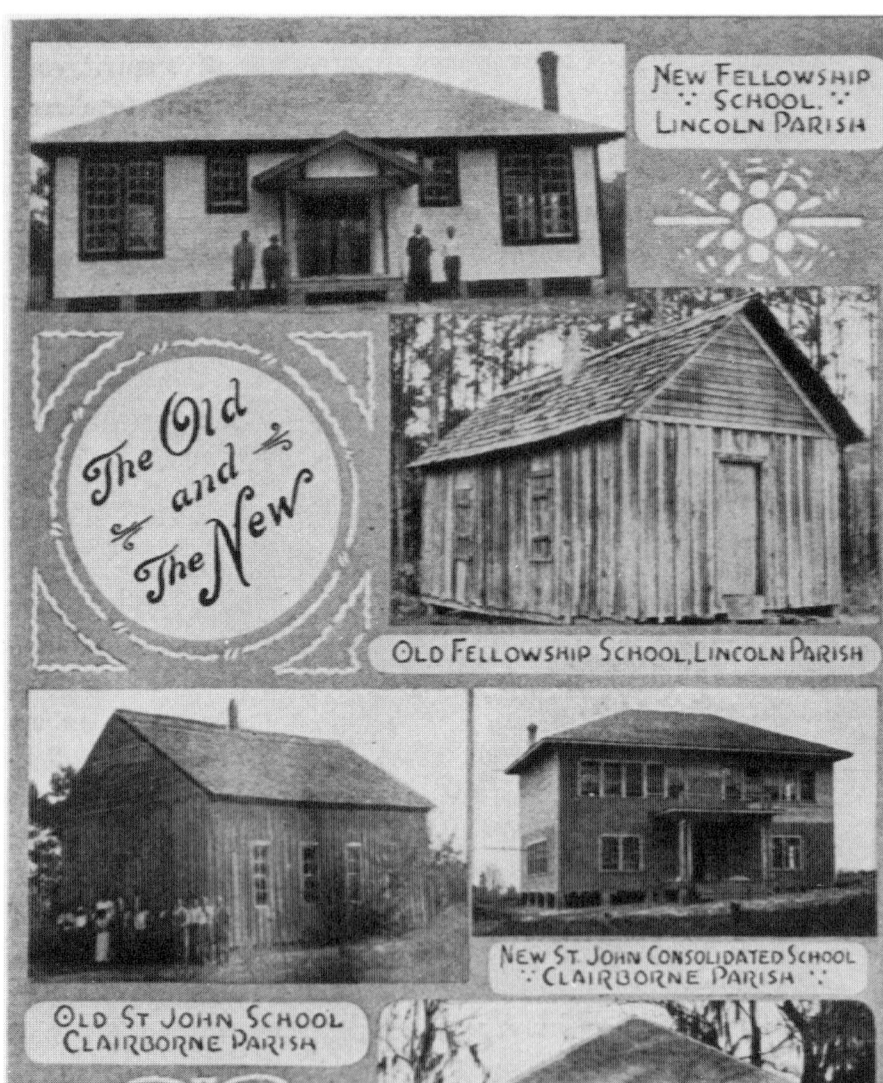

NEW FELLOWSHIP SCHOOL, LINCOLN PARISH

The Old and The New

OLD FELLOWSHIP SCHOOL, LINCOLN PARISH

NEW ST. JOHN CONSOLIDATED SCHOOL, CLAIRBORNE PARISH

OLD ST JOHN SCHOOL, CLAIRBORNE PARISH

NEW WILDSVILLE SCHOOL, CONCORDIA PARISH

OLD WILDSVILLE SCHOOL, CONCORDIA PARISH

by personal solicitation, meetings, church functions, raffles and other community efforts.

Communities made great sacrifices in order to obtain a school. Money was raised by selling eggs, hens, corn, cotton, berries and other produce. Some people pledged their cows and calves, and children pledged their saved pennies. In one village farmers committed a small area of land planted in cotton, which they called "The Rosenwald Patch," and donated the proceeds to the school fund. In another town in Alabama, one man who had been a slave emptied out his life's savings of $38 ($567) in nickels, dimes, and pennies. "I want to see the children and grandchildren have a chance, so I am giving all I have," he told the meeting. The Tuskegee representative expected to raise $10, but the town collected $1,365 ($18,000). Subsequently, this community, with the aid of Rosenwald, built a school costing $10,000 ($72,000), employing five teachers, and serving hundreds of students.

Dr. Washington's support for the school project was vital in building confidence in the minds of both Whites and Blacks that the plan was sound. In fact, schools were not built in communities where there was strong antagonism, White or Black. There was the chance that Blacks would not maintain the schools. Also, there was the danger that schoolhouses would be burned down by Whites.

The land for each schoolhouse was deeded to the local school authorities, and the completed building became part of the public school system. When schools were completed they were inspected by the state superintendent of education, who reported to the officials of the Rosenwald Fund. Rosenwald required a guarantee that the schools would be operated for a minimum of five consecutive months during the year. For the first six experimental schools, Rosenwald contributed to each a total of just under $2,000 ($30,000) and the local Blacks, in addition to some Whites and the state, contributed more than $3,000 ($44,775). When Rosenwald visited these first

CHILDREN'S DAY PROGRAM

PREPARED AND ARRANGED BY

Sunday School Deptment C. M. E. Church

Six Teacher Rosenwald School
This building has been constructed in fourteen Southern States and costs from $8,000.00 to $10,000.00

J. A. MARTIN, Editor,
123 14th Avenue North, Nashville, Tenn.

schools he was so impressed with the potential of the plan that he decided to give Dr. Washington another $30,000 ($434,000) for the construction of 100 additional schools, which were now being called "Rosenwald Schools."

Dr. Washington died in 1915. He was mourned by many Americans and Rosenwald established a $100,000 ($1.4 million) fund in his memory. Rosenwald also gave $250,000 ($3.5 million) to Tuskegee's endowment.

By then the Rosenwald schools had begun to receive national attention, and many Southern states were shamed into giving Black education more financial support. In 1916 the State of Alabama passed legislation offering state aid for rural schoolhouse construction for Blacks to the extent of half the amount raised by local communities. Under this plan the state contributed $300 ($4,286), the local community $300, and Rosenwald $300 for a school with one teacher.

Rosenwald was so pleased with the project that in 1916 he offered to pay one-third of the cost of an additional 300 rural schoolhouses in the South. He also organized a conference on schoolhouse construction, gathering together many important participants in this field. He urged adoption of an extensive, orderly plan for construction of a large number of Black schools in all the Southern states. Other states in the South began to apply for Rosenwald's aid, and in time all of the Southern States were participating in the project. The headquarters were expanded and moved from Tuskegee to Nashville. The plan became too large for Rosenwald to run by himself. As noted earlier, in 1917 he formed the Julius Rosenwald Fund as a clearing house for some of his larger projects, such as the Southern School Building program.

Under the enlarged school construction plan, the Fund stipulated that money would only be furnished for rural schoolhouses in localities where the school term was at least five consecutive months and for teachers' homes where the school term was eight months or more. Every community that wanted a school had to guarantee enough land for playgrounds and for agricultural work where it was deemed necessary. Labor, land and materials furnished locally were counted as cash at current market values. The communities also had to guarantee to equip, furnish, and maintain the schools. The objective was to gradually decrease contributions from the Rosenwald Fund and other individuals and to increase public support, in the hope that the whole project would eventually be taken over with government funds.

Sometimes unbelievable odds had to be overcome for these schools to be built. John Culkin, superintendent of the Warren County, Mississippi schools, was disturbed by the lack of decent Black schools and applied for Rosenwald funding; the Fund agreed to aid in the construction of 25 new schools in the various Black communities within the county.

However, the Superintendent had a problem more serious than financing the building. He knew the Ku Klux Klan would attempt to stop construction because of their opposition to improving Black education. In order to keep the Klan from obtaining injunctions in local courts to halt construction, Mr. Culkin ordered the entire program be initiated at the same moment in each community and with the utmost secrecy.

There followed a tremendous amount of organizational activity. Specifications and complete lists of materials for all of the schools reached lumber mills along with orders that the lumber, earmarked for each school, must be at the appropriate railroad station on a specified morning. The cooperation of leading White citizens in each community was secured. They not only agreed to make contributions of money but to provide mule teams and wagons to haul the lumber from the rail station to the site of each school. Early on a Monday morning, when freight cars loaded with lumber pulled into the rail yard, 160 mule teams and wagons were on hand to deliver the building materials to the various communities. There, workmen had already laid the foundation, and building began at once. Women and children, under the leadership of teachers, had been organized in teams. The children worked on the school sites, cleaning and grading the play area and making walk-ways, while Black women's clubs served hot lunches to the laborers. The foremen and carpenters worked in a desperate rush, urged on by the superintendent, who sped tirelessly from school to school giving directions. Within a week all 25 of the buildings were enclosed and roofed. Within a month each had been completed, painted inside and out, equipped, and was ready for use.

In the meantime, knowing that injunction proceedings were being prepared to stop the construction, Mr. Culkin stayed out of reach so that no warrant could be served. When the sheriff finally found him, it was too late. "The buildings are done," the superintendent said, "and we have already paid for the materials and most of the labor." The Klan reluctantly dropped the injunction proceedings and was warned by the White community leaders that the new schools should not be harmed.

Beyond Schools:
Rosenwald Libraries, Buses, and Fellowships

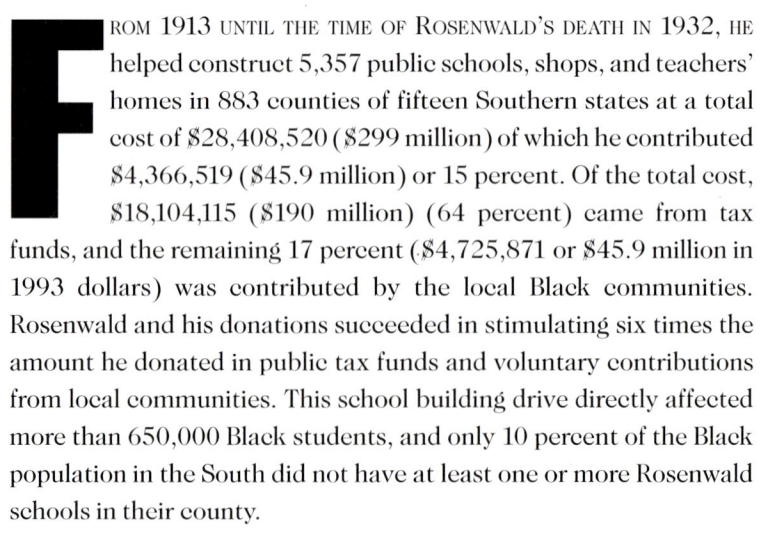

▼

FROM 1913 UNTIL THE TIME OF ROSENWALD'S DEATH IN 1932, HE helped construct 5,357 public schools, shops, and teachers' homes in 883 counties of fifteen Southern states at a total cost of $28,408,520 ($299 million) of which he contributed $4,366,519 ($45.9 million) or 15 percent. Of the total cost, $18,104,115 ($190 million) (64 percent) came from tax funds, and the remaining 17 percent ($4,725,871 or $45.9 million in 1993 dollars) was contributed by the local Black communities. Rosenwald and his donations succeeded in stimulating six times the amount he donated in public tax funds and voluntary contributions from local communities. This school building drive directly affected more than 650,000 Black students, and only 10 percent of the Black population in the South did not have at least one or more Rosenwald schools in their county.

In order not to create excessive dependency on Rosenwald aid by Southern states, the Fund ended the school construction program soon after Rosenwald's death in 1933. Without a doubt, Rosenwald's hopes and expectations for the program had been realized. States and the communities were finally paying attention to the serious problem of Black education. For example, in 1931, public tax funds met 72 percent of the cost of school construction for Blacks as contrasted with the first five years of the program when only 17 percent of the money came from public sources. Illiteracy was still a major problem in the South, but at least now the issue was not ignored as it had been in the past and some effective tools had been created to address the situation. During and after the school construction program, the Fund gave increased attention to initiating other programs to improve the Black educational system.

The Fund took an interest in consolidated schools. It was evident that counties would need help in providing transportation to bring rural students to a central location; there were not enough buses for Blacks. The Fund therefore agreed to contribute toward the establishment of bus transportation, supplying half the cost of the bus itself and part of the operating expense for three years. This contribution was made on condition that the county authorities agreed to assume full responsibility at the end of the three-year period, that the length of the school term would be not less than eight months, and that no teacher in the school would be paid less than $60 a month. The Fund helped provide 270 buses, which transported ten thousand Black students eight thousand miles daily in 128 counties of thirteen Southern states.

In a further effort to bring Black schools up to a standard eight- or nine-month term, the Fund offered to help pay toward the cost of extending terms by one or two months, with the understanding that the total cost, after three years, would be provided by public tax funds.

ROSENWALD DAY
County-Wide Celebration
MARCH 22nd, 1929

The State Board of Education, through Mr. W. D. Gresham, State Agent, has decreed, beginning March 1st, 1929 to March 30th, that some day be set aside in each county known as Rosenwald Day on which day all schools in the County shall observe by an appropriate celebration. March 22 has been designated in Brunswick County as ROSENWALD DAY.

As President of the Brunswick School League and Teachers' Association, with the approval of Division Supt. Chambliss, I am requesting each teacher in the county to observe the day by presenting the official program sent from Richmond. This is required. I am also asking that people in each school community attend the meeting to show their appreciation of Mr. Rosenwald's interest in us, which has enabled our county to build more Rosenwald Schools than any county in the State (15) in number. All told Mr. Rosenwald has contributed $10,000 to this county for better schools and if we add his contribution of $10,000 to the Elementary School of St. Paul's which is also public, it will make a total of $20,000 for the education of our children. Surely we can honor such a benefactor.

Therefore at 2 p. m. Friday, MARCH 22, 1929, Teachers, Pupils and Parents in each community will assemble in their respective school or church of the community, if the school be unsuitable, and celebrate the day.

James S. Russell, President
W. H. Haines, Secretary and Supervisor
(Mrs.) Ophelia Haines, Supervisor

R. Lee Chambliss——Div. Superintendent

Libraries

▼

THE FUND SUPPORTED NUMEROUS OTHER PROJECTS, INCLUDING A library service that supplied reading materials to rural schools, Black colleges, and community libraries. The rural schools program continued for twelve years, during which more than half a million books were distributed to schools throughout the Southern states. About 60 percent of the books went to one- and two-room schools and the remainder to Southern towns with a population of less than 2,500.

The value of these books to small schools and communities cannot be exaggerated. In 1928 only two states in the South provided free textbooks; many rural children could not afford to buy books and more than half the rural Black school population was without the simplest materials of instruction. For them, the books in Rosenwald libraries were the only volumes of any sort available for use either in or out of school.

In 1927 the scarcity of books in Black colleges and teaching institutions was as desperate as in the rural communities. Clearly, these institutions of higher learning could not fulfill their function without adequate libraries. A large portion of the limited books available were

LIBRARIES

decrepit theology and history volumes given by missionary groups as charity. Even where there was an adequate book collection, librarians frequently were poorly trained.

To stimulate an improvement in college libraries, the Fund offered to contribute one-third of the cost of books that were on a list created by Hampton Normal and Agricultural Institute, up to a maximum of $2,500 ($26,000). By time the program ended in 1934, forty-three colleges in sixteen states had received aid totaling $54,000 ($580,000). Even though the sum was relatively small, it stimulated an interest in library development that led colleges, with the aid of cooperating agencies, to attract an investment of more than $2 million ($210 million), and this library development helped colleges qualify for state accreditation.

Also, many communities in the South had been unable to furnish adequate public library facilities. In 1928, 71 percent of this population was entirely without a public or county library. Of the 8.5 million Blacks in thirteen Southern states, 7.5 million were without public libraries of any kind.

The Fund assisted central libraries in county seats and branch library stations in schools, churches, stores and individuals homes. Book trucks touring the counties maintained a constant exchange of books among the branch stations and also served individual readers.

Teacher Education

▼

D URING THE COURSE OF THE SCHOOL-BUILDING PROGRAM, THE Fund also actively developed programs and institutions that improved teacher education programs in the Black South in an effort to enhance the quality of education. Rural school teachers had little education or training and were poorly paid. Salaries were so low that the only teachers willing to stay were those unable to obtain posts in the cities. The typical teacher had only a high school graduation certificate. The Fund sought to change this situation by providing the kind of education designed to prepare the teachers more fully to meet their responsibilities. It also aimed at encouraging well-qualified teachers to make their careers in rural education, while enabling the public school system to assist in setting up such a system.

The Fund spent more than $1.6 million ($17.2-million) on teacher education. This program comprised large grants to teacher training institutions and smaller amounts for supplementary reading materials, conferences, and surveys.

Higher Education

▼

THE FUND'S MAJOR EFFORT IN HIGHER EDUCATION FOR BLACKS WAS focused on four universities strategically placed throughout the Southern states: Washington, D.C. (Howard University), Atlanta (The Confederated Institute), Nashville (Fisk University), and New Orleans (Dillard University). For example, the Rosenwald Fund contributions enabled Howard University to acquire much-needed land for growth and supported its Department of Biology under the renowned scientist E.E. Just. Along with the Federal government, the Fund played an active role in Howard University's development. Knowing the Fund itself would soon cease to exist, its board set up the United Negro College Fund, which was started by the Rosenwald Fund along with other institutions in 1944.

The Rosenwald Fellowships program had a sizable impact on a generation of highly talented Blacks and Whites who wished to study in institutions such as Harvard and Yale or who aspired to go abroad for study. The fellowships were open to Blacks of unusual talent and ability in any field and to a few equally able White Southerners who wished to work on a problem distinctive to the South and who planned to pursue their careers in the South. Almost $2 million ($21.5 million) were given to more than 1,500 people. The recipient list reads like a *Who's Who* of Black America: W.E.B Du Bois for creative writing, Ralph Bunche for international relations, Ralph Ellison for creative writing, Zora Hurston for anthropology, and Marian Anderson for music.

Hospitals

▼

THE ROSENWALD FUND ALSO FOCUSED ATTENTION ON HEALTH care. By making substantial contributions to numerous Black hospitals that offered training opportunities, the Fund helped open medicine to Black doctors and nurses. In 1928 there were only fourteen Black public health nurses in the entire South outside Alabama, and most of them were poorly trained. In three years the number increased to over 35, and many new student nurses and doctors had entered these newly-funded medical training facilities.

Conclusion

▼

JULIUS ROSENWALD RANKS AMONG THE GREAT PHILANTHROPISTS IN U.S. history even though he is not as well recognized as Rockefeller and Carnegie who had more money and set up larger foundations. Despite this, Rosenwald's Fund was so wisely conceived, administered, and targeted that it had the most substantial influence on the Black community over the years. In sum, Rosenwald gave as much, if not more, thought and effort to his philanthropies as he did to his business.

Rosenwald himself said his dedication to helping Blacks was because he was a Jew and the tragic experiences of many Jews had given him a sympathetic understanding of other persecuted peoples. He was also interested in American Blacks because he was an American who cherished the ideals of democracy and who did not see how America could go forward if a large segment of the population were left behind. *The Crisis*, the NAACP's and W.E.B. Du Bois's monthly journal, quoted a Chicago banker at the dedication of a Rosenwald YMCA: "Mr. Rosenwald's gift will stimulate the race throughout the country. It will furnish many centers from which will radiate not only fresh hope but powerful educative and uplifting

CONCLUSION

forces. I do not hesitate to say that Mr. Rosenwald's gift will prove to be the most important benefaction the colored race has received since the Emancipation Proclamation."

Rosenwald hoped for sweeping changes in race relations and clearly recognized that much more needed to be done. He offered leadership and resources and helped chart the direction of change. From the beginning, almost all of Rosenwald's work had a bearing on race relations: the building of rural schoolhouses, the education of teachers, the improvement of Black colleges and universities, the development of health services, and the award of fellowships. These programs looked toward the growth of that group of the population that had been most neglected. What would he say about race relations, especially Black-Jewish relations, today?

Appendix A (1)

▼

Rosenwald's Donations in Today's Dollars

by Robert M. Solow
MIT Professor and Nobel Laureate in Economics

WE KNOW THAT JULIUS ROSENWALD GAVE AWAY ABOUT $63 MILLION between 1911 and 1932, more in the last decade than in the first. To appreciate the magnitude of his contribution, we have to translate that sum into current terms. A dollar in 1921 would buy goods worth roughly $8 in 1933. Rosenwald's $63 million represents much more than that in purchase-powering terms today. No exact translation is possible, if only because we do not know the exact annual pattern of his donations. Even if we did, no such comparison can carry complete conviction over a span of 80 years. But it is better to make an approximate translation than none at all.

Suppose we assume that one-third of the $63 million was given away between 1911 and 1921, and the remaining two-thirds between 1921 and 1932. If we use the consumer price index to convert these into 1993 equivalents, we should multiply the earlier donations by

Rosenwald's Donations in Today's Dollars

something like 13.33 and the later ones by about 8.33. That is because prices have risen more since 1916, say, than since 1927. On that basis, Rosenwald's $63 million would be worth roughly ten times as much—$630 million—in dollars of 1993 purchasing power.

That is a large sum, but it probably underestimates the extent of Rosenwald's generosity. The United States was a much poorer community during the second and third decades of this century than it has become in the tenth decade. It would be more enlightening to make a conversion based on income levels. Instead of asking how many chocolate bars and shoes Rosenwald gave away, one could ask instead how many years worth of an average person's income did he give away. That precise question cannot be answered. But we can do almost as well by asking: How many hours of an average person's labor are represented by Rosenwald's donations?

Wage comparisons are possible, although data for the early part of the century are sketchy. The average hourly earnings of production workers in manufacturing in 1914 came to 22 cents. By 1929 the wage had risen to 56 cents. In 1993, the corresponding figure is $11.74. If we use those wage rates to make the conversion, Rosenwald's $63 million translates into roughly $2 billion in 1993. It should be clear what this means. If we think not in terms of purchasing power over goods but purchasing power over hours of average labor, Rosenwald gave away $2 billion in today's terms.

There is one other adjustment that should be mentioned, although it cannot be made. When charitable donations are deductible from income for tax purposes, any dollar given costs the donor less when (marginal) tax rates are high than when they are low. If there were no income tax, it would cost a dollar to give a dollar. For anyone in the 50 percent bracket, the gift of a deductible dollar costs the donor 50 cents; the other 50 cents is matching gift from the U.S. Treasury. Income tax rates in the

Rosenwald's Donations in Today's Dollars

United States. have varied. The top bracket rate was seven percent in 1913-1915, 77 percent in 1918, back down to 25 percent in 1925-1928, as high as 94 percent during the Second World War, a little over 70 percent in 1970, and 40 percent now. It is hard to escape the impression that Rosenwald lived and gave in an era of lower tax rates (though deductibility rules may have changed as well). In that case, his after-tax effort was even greater than the figures given above would suggest.

Appendix A (2)

▼

Consumer Price Index

	1982-84 = 100	1993 = 100	1900 = 100
1910	9.3	6.4	112.0
1911	9.3	6.4	112.0
1912	9.7	6.7	116.9
1913	9.9	6.9	119.3
1914	10.0	6.9	120.5
1915	10.1	7.0	121.7
1916	10.9	7.5	131.3
1917	12.8	8.9	154.2
1918	15.1	10.4	181.9
1919	17.3	12.0	208.4
1920	20.0	13.8	241.0
1921	17.9	12.4	215.7
1922	16.8	11.6	202.4
1923	17.1	11.8	206.0
1924	17.1	11.8	206.0
1925	17.5	12.1	210.8
1926	17.7	12.2	213.3
1927	17.4	12.0	209.6
1928	17.1	11.8	206.0
1929	17.1	11.8	206.0
1930	16.7	11.6	201.2
1931	15.2	10.5	183.1
1932	13.7	9.5	165.1

Appendix B

▼

Location of Rosenwald YMCAs

City	Branch	Date Opened
Washington, DC	12th St.	1912
Chicago, IL	Wabash	1913
Indianapolis, IN	Senate Ave.	1913
Philadelphia, PA	Christian St.	1914
Kansas City, MO	Paseo Department	1914
Cincinnati, OH	9th St.	1914
Brooklyn, NY	Carlton Ave.	1918
Baltimore, MD	Druid Hill Ave.	1919
St. Louis, MO	Pine St.	1919
Columbus, OH	Spring St.	1919
New York, NY	135th St.	1919
Atlanta, GA	Butler St.	1920
Pittsburgh, PA	Centre Ave.	1923
Denver, CO	Glenarm Branch	1924
Detroit, MI	St. Antoine	1925
Los Angeles, CA	28th St.	1926
Buffalo, NY	Michigan Ave.	1928
Dayton, OH	5th St.	1928
Montclair, NJ	Washington St.	1928
Toledo, OH	Indiana Ave.	1930
Youngstown, OH	West Federal St.	1931
Orange, NJ	Oakwood Ave.	1932
Harrisburg, PA	Forster St.	1933

Appendix C

▼

Endorsements

Professor Russell Adams,
Chairman Afro-American Studies,
Howard University

■

Julian Bond
Distinguished Adjunct Professor of Government

■

Hyman Bookbinder
Washington Representative Emeritus
American Jewish Committee

■

Abraham H. Foxman
National Director
Anti-Defamation League

■

William H. Gray, III
President
United Negro College Fund, Inc.

■

Representative John Lewis
Georgia, 5th District

■

Chuck Morgan
Advocate for Equal Rights

■

Hugh Price
President, National Urban League

■

Bill Rosenwald
Julius Rosenwald's surviving son

ENDORSEMENTS

The history of relations between the Black and Jewish communities in America is multidimensional, rich, and complex. In a nation where events move quickly and memories are short, the story of "A School in Every County—The Partnership of Jewish Philanthropist Julius Rosenwald and American Black Communities" brings a significant aspect of the Black-Jewish relationship to life. While it is difficult today to comprehend the nearly total disenfranchisement during the first half of the twentieth century of Southern black children from their most basic right and necessity—the right to a decent education—it is equally inspiring to understand how Black communities across the South, with the pivotal assistance of a Jewish businessman from Chicago, stepped into the breach. They joined hands around a value and need so basic to each community's traditions, and left a legacy that is written in the lives of millions and in the enduring work of the United Negro College Fund. If Blacks and Jews—indeed, all Americans—are to find ways in the future to jointly address America's problems, it is essential that they become aware of shared history such as this wonderful recounting of the story of the partnership of American Black Communities and the great philanthropist, Julius Rosenwald.

Abraham H. Foxman
National Director
Anti-Defamation League

A solid and illuminating treatment of this aspect of American history. The Rosenwald African-American school construction project was an important confluence of two groups with a profound interest in the power of education for social change and group uplift.

Professor Russell Adams,
Chairman Afro-American Studies
Howard University

Endorsements

Until now, little was known of the unique and enduring role of Julius Rosenwald in supporting equal opportunity for Black Americans during an era of segregation, persecution, and social inequality. Not only did Mr. Rosenwald help found the United Negro College Fund, he also supported hundreds of schools for black children, helped to strengthen many historically black colleges, and provided books for schools and communities in the rural South. Mr. Rosenwald understood ahead of his time that the future of America was inextricably bound by the educational future of its most disadvantaged citizens. Thanks to "A School in Every County—The Partnership of Jewish Philanthropist Julius Rosenwald and American Black Communities," we now understand the pioneering trail that Mr. Rosenwald blazed.

William H. Gray, III
President
United Negro College Fund, Inc.

This account of Julius Rosenwald's extraordinary contribution to the "relentless crusade against race prejudice" that he advocated all his life is a much-needed addition to the record of positive, mutually-enriching co-operation between American Jews and American Blacks. It can serve as a valuable teaching tool especially for young Jews and young Blacks who are often uninformed about the glorious history of Black-Jewish co-operation and understanding.

Hyman Bookbinder
Washington Representative Emeritus
American Jewish Committee

Endorsements

A valuable look at an interesting and little known chapter in the history of the relationship between Blacks and Jews. Blacks and Jews fought together on the civil rights battlefield. Julius Rosenwald's philanthropy educated half a generation of Southern Black schoolchildren and a Who's Who of the Black intellectual elite earlier. This story needs to be read.

> *Julian Bond*
> *Distinguished Adjunct Professor of*
> *Government, The American University*
> *Lecturer in History, The University*
> *of Virginia*

The National Urban League is especially proud to endorse this excellent monograph describing Julius Rosenwald's dedication to Black Education. He was greatly influenced by a biography of William Baldwin, Jr., a founder of the Urban League. His contributions to the establishment of schools for Blacks in the segregated South of the early 20th century, parallels the Urban League's current effort on training and employment.

> *Hugh Price*
> *President*
> *National Urban League*

Two unlikely partners, a Jewish businessman and philanthropist, Julius Rosenwald, and a man born in slavery, Booker T. Washington, formed a unique partnership more than seventy years ago to help Blacks achieve educational equality. It is a story that needs telling. This monograph does it wonderfully.

> *Representative John Lewis*
> *Georgia, 5th District*

ENDORSEMENTS

A little bit of land and labor were what Black folks needed to get Julius Rosenwald's money for a school. From those schools came the parents of the generation who marched and sang and risked their lives in the revolution for equal justice under the law.

Charles Morgan, Jr.
Advocate for Equal Rights

Highest congratulations on, and warmest appreciation for your excellent monogram on Dad. It was an inspiration and an eye opener for me, and gave me new appreciation for Dad's wonderful character and motivations.

Bill Rosenwald
Julius Rosenwald's surviving son

Bibliography

▼

Primary Source
The Papers of Julius Rosenwald in the Department of Special Collections, University of Chicago Library.

Periodicals
The Crisis. New York: National Association for the Advancement of Colored People.

Opportunity. New York: National Urban League.

Secondary Sources
Angell, Pauline. "Julius Rosenwald." *American Jewish Year Book*, Vol. 34, 1933: pp. 141-176.

Bachmann, Lawrence P. "Julius Rosenwald." *American Jewish History Quarterly*, Vol. 66, no. 1, 1976: pp. 89-105.

Brooks, John Graham. *An American Citizen, the Life of William Henry Baldwin, Jr.* Boston: Houghton Mifflin, 1910.

Embree, Edward and Julia Waxman. *Investment in People: The Story of the Julius Rosenwald Fund.* New York: Harper and Brothers, 1949.

Jarrette, Alfred. *Julius Rosenwald: Benefactor of Mankind.* Greenville, South Carolina: Southeastern University Press, 1975.

Mjagkij, Nina. "A Peculiar Alliance: Julius Rosenwald, the YMCA, and African-Americans, 1910-1933." *American Jewish Archives*, Vol. 44, no. 2, Fall/Winter 1992: pp. 585-607.

Washington, Booker T. *Up From Slavery, An Autobiography.* New York: Doubleday, 1901.

Werner, Morris. *Julius Rosenwald: The Life of a Practical Humanitarian.* New York: Harper and Brothers, 1939.

Acknowledgments

▼

THIS MONOGRAPH WAS WRITTEN BY JEFFREY SOSLAND AND WAS sponsored by the Goldmuntz Family who were made aware of Rosenwald's pioneering efforts by veteran civil rights advocate, Chuck Morgan. Lawrence Goldmuntz, Stephen Kurzman of the American Jewish Committee, Peter Ascoli—a Rosenwald descendent, William Rosenwald—Julius Rosenwald's surviving son, and MIT Professor and Nobel Laureate in Economics, Robert M. Solow, contributed to the preparation of this draft. The Department of Special Collections at the University of Chicago's Regenstein Library provided research assistance for this monograph, the graphics, and photos.